The insights shared in this book are intended to be catalysts to get your mind thinking about the movement you have within you. If you want to get a bigger picture of what your movement really is and how these concepts tie together in a larger framework, I'd love to give you a free copy to the blueprint on How To Start A Movement.

JosephRanseth.com/aha

Go Ahead, Start A Movement

Insights to Help You Take Your Message to the World

Joseph Ranseth

THiNKaha®

An Actionable Business Journal

E-mail: info@thinkaha.com
20660 Stevens Creek Blvd., Suite 210
Cupertino, CA 95014

Published by THiNKaha®
20660 Stevens Creek Blvd., Suite 210, Cupertino, CA 95014
http://thinkaha.com
E-mail: info@thinkaha.com

First Printing: March 2018
Hardcover ISBN: 978-1-61699-258-3   1-61699-258-1
Paperback ISBN: 978-1-61699-257-6   1-61699-257-3
eBook ISBN: 978-1-61699-259-0   1-61699-259-X
Place of Publication: Silicon Valley, California, USA
Paperback Library of Congress Number: 2018902276

Trademarks

Warning and Disclaimer

Acknowledgements

The world is full of dreamers and change-makers, who are living lives dedicated to serving other people, their local communities, and the planet as a whole. I honor your contribution and the inspiration you are to me and my work, as well as the rest of the world. Keep up the amazing work, it's why you're here.

Dedication

For Winter, your courage and contribution inspire me every day.

For Enoch, your smile reminds me that good is always present.

How to Read a THiNKaha® Book
A Note from the Publisher

The THiNKaha series is the CliffsNotes of the 21st century. The value of these books is that they are contextual in nature. Although the actual words won't change, their meaning will change every time you read one as your context will change. Experience your own "AHA!" moments ("AHAmessages™") with a THiNKaha book; AHAmessages are looked at as "actionable" moments—think of a specific project you're working on, an event, a sales deal, a personal issue, etc. and see how the AHAmessages in this book can inspire your own AHAmessages, something that you can specifically act on. Here's how to read one of these books and have it work for you:

1. Read a THiNKaha book (these slim and handy books should only take about 15–20 minutes of your time!) and write down one to three actionable items you thought of while reading it. Each journal-style THiNKaha book is equipped with space for you to write down your notes and thoughts underneath each AHAmessage.

2. Mark your calendar to re-read this book again in 30 days.

3. Repeat step #1 and write down one to three more AHAmessages that grab you this time. I guarantee that they will be different than the first time. BTW: this is also a great time to reflect on the actions taken from the last set of AHAmessages you wrote down.

After reading a THiNKaha book, writing down your AHAmessages, re-reading it, and writing down more AHAmessages, you'll begin to see how these books contextually apply to you. THiNKaha books advocate for continuous, lifelong learning. They will help you transform your ahas into actionable items with tangible results until you no longer have to say "AHA!" to these moments—they'll become part of your daily practice as you continue to grow and learn.

As The AHA Guy at THiNKaha, I definitely practice what I preach. I read 2-3 AHAbooks a month in addition to those that we publish and take away two to three different action items from each of them every time. Please e-mail me your AHAs today!

Mitchell Levy
publisher@thinkaha.com

THiNK*aha*®

Contents

Introduction

There is an inner yearning within each of us. A faint but powerful whisper telling us that there's something more. That we're destined to have a bigger impact than we're having now. A voice that once expressed, will inspire others to their own greatness and in a very profound way, make the world better. This is your movement, and if you've ever felt a pull that you could be having a bigger impact, then you know that life is calling your movement to come out from within you. This is why you are here.

The content in this book is based on the Take Your Message to the World™ framework developed by Joseph Ranseth and used by his clients around the world. For nearly fifteen years, Joseph has been helping people transform their lives and organizations using the blueprint and principles that transformational leaders such as Gandhi and Dr. King used to change the world. As a sought-after speaker and transformational coach, Joseph is on a mission to "transform the transformers" by empowering authors, speakers, coaches, and other purpose-driven entrepreneurs with the tools they need to increase their reach and impact and to move their business beyond transactions to transformation.

Take your time with the material in this book. Reflect on it and allow yourself to open up to a greater degree of impact that you know you were put here to have.

Go ahead, start a movement.

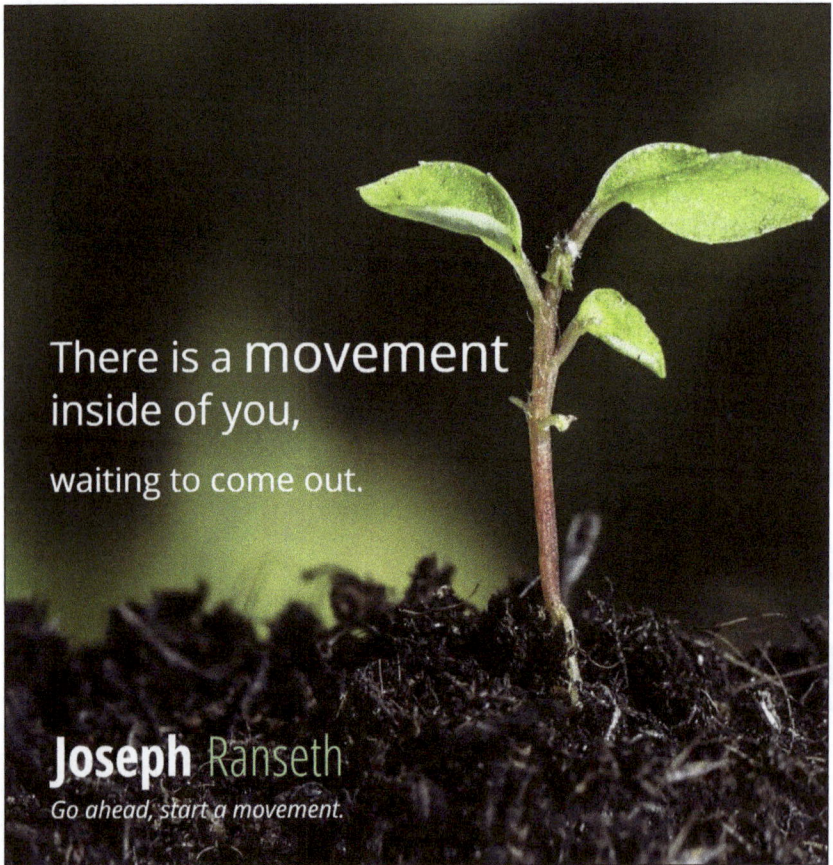

There is a **movement** inside of you,

waiting to come out.

Joseph Ranseth

Go ahead, start a movement.

Share the AHA messages from this book socially by going to
http://aha.pub/StartAMovement.

Section I

You Have A Movement

There is an inner whisper inside of you telling you that you have a message and a mission to share with the world. When you listen to that voice and align with your true source of power, you can turn that message into a movement. This book outlines the steps to do just that.

Go ahead, start a movement.

1

There is an inner yearning within each of us: a faint but powerful whisper that tells us that there's something more, that we're destined to have a bigger impact than we do now.

_____

_____

_____

2

Listening and acting upon your inner voice inspires others to their own greatness and in a very tangible way, makes the world better.

_____

_____

_____

3

You were put here to do something meaningful. That meaningful thing is your personal movement.

_____

_____

_____

4

How do you know that the world needs you? Because you're here.

_____

_____

_____

5

If you had 1 minute and the entire world's attention, what would you want to share? This might be a clue to your movement.

_____

_____

_____

6

You were put here to do something far more important than simply make a living. You have a movement worth living for.

_____

_____

_____

7

We change the world not by what we do, but by who we become.

_____

_____

_____

8

There is a spark of greatness within you. Your movement is what happens when you fan it into a flame.

_____

_____

_____

9

The cause inside of you is far more fulfilling than any amount of applause.

_____

_____

_____

10

Your life will be remembered not because of what you have, but because of what you gave.

_____

_____

_____

11

Honor the inner whisper.
It sees your greatness even when you can't.
It will guide you to your movement.

_____

_____

_____

12

We don't create impact by making ourselves significant;
we become significant because of the
impact we make on others.

_____

_____

_____

13

The capacity to touch the life of another human being is
unlocked by being fully present.

_____

_____

_____

14

Want to change the world? Ask yourself, "How can I serve in this moment?", a thousand times a day.

_____

_____

_____

15

Your movement is not determined by the size of your reach, it's determined by the measure of your impact.

_____

_____

_____

16

Marketing is about creating transactions;
a movement is about creating transformation.

_____

_____

_____

17

Transformation is a change in how people see themselves, others, and the world around them.

_____

_____

_____

18

Who you are is greater than your thoughts and feelings. Seeing this is freedom. Helping others to see it can spark a movement.

_____

_____

_____

19

Your movement can start with any act that helps others see and believe in a new or greater possibility for their lives.

_____

_____

_____

20

Small actions, consistently taken, will change the course of history. Live your movement in even the simple moments.

_____

_____

_____

21

If you could teach the world one lesson before you died, what would it be?

_____

_____

_____

22

When we see the world through a lens of love, nearly every change we aspire to see will happen as a by-product.

_____

_____

_____

23

Peace in the world is the product of peace in enough people's hearts. How does your movement cultivate peace in others?

_____

_____

_____

24

The world doesn't need us to change it, it needs us to change the way we see it. Your movement will give others a new lens through which they see life.

_____

_____

_____

Let your adversities
refine you,

not define you.

Joseph Ranseth
Go ahead, start a movement.

Share the AHA messages from this book socially by going to
http://aha.pub/StartAMovement.

Section II

Arriving Through Adversity

Gandhi didn't liberate India from a vacuum, and Dr. King didn't take up the cause of civil rights just because he was bored. They started their movements because there was an adversity facing them and their communities. In a similar way, the adversities we face in our individual lives plant the seed for the gift that we can bring to the world to create transformation.

As you read this section, take note that the adversity in your life isn't an obstacle to your movement, it is your movement.

25

The obstacles you face in life aren't getting in the way of your personal movement, they ARE your movement.

_____

_____

_____

26

Gandhi & Dr. King didn't become heroes because they had the strength to overcome their adversities; they knew how to transform adversities into strength to do even greater things.

_____

_____

_____

27

Transforming your own adversity into something beautiful elevates the consciousness of the planet.

_____

_____

_____

28

Embracing your adversities is a transformative gift to the planet.

_____

_____

_____

29

If it stirs an emotion, it carries a lesson.

_____

_____

_____

30

Performance = potential - resistance.

_____

_____

_____

31

Things do NOT happen for a reason. They happen,
then we get to choose the reason.

_____

_____

_____

32

Enlightenment: Life gives us things so we can give them back.

_____

_____

_____

33

Embrace your adversities, and use them as a gift of service to the rest of the planet.

_____

_____

_____

34

Don't settle to simply overcome your adversity;
commit to transforming it and giving back to others
as an act of service.

_____

_____

_____

35

Shit happens. Will you wallow in it or use it as fertilizer?

_____

_____

_____

36

Adversity is the refining fire to remove the impurities that stand in the way of you living your movement to its full expression.

_____

_____

_____

37

Just because you don't feel the sun doesn't mean it isn't there. The clouds remind us of the ebb and flow of life.

_____

_____

_____

38

Instead of seeing your failures as weakness, realize they are opportunities to develop your strength and increase your capacity.

_____

_____

_____

39

Everything in life is serving a singular purpose:
to show you who you truly are.

_____

_____

_____

40

As a seed needs water and sunshine, your soul's movement requires challenge and purification.

_____

_____

_____

41

Nothing is in the way of your purpose. What you are facing is a part of your purpose.

_____

_____

_____

42

Nothing in life is happening to you. It's happening for you. Your movement is calling you to embrace it.

_____

_____

_____

43

Recipe for Compassion: People work perfectly. People make the best choices available to them. Underlying every behavior is a positive intention.

_____

_____

_____

44

The problem is never "out there." Everything is pointing you to where the truth is: inside.

_____

_____

_____

45

The strong don't avoid mistakes. They embrace them
and grow from them.

_____

_____

_____

46

Instead of complaining, ask: "How does this serve me
and my movement?"

_____

_____

_____

47

The best way to get rid of an enemy is to make it your friend -- this includes your adversities.

_____

_____

_____

48

Gratitude is only a half measure if it's only for the good things in our lives.

_____

_____

_____

49

Your shortcomings don't diminish your greatness,
they accentuate it.

_____

_____

_____

50

"Where you stumble, there lies treasure. The cave you're afraid to enter is the source of what you're looking for. The damned thing in the cave, so dreaded, has become the center." -- Joseph Campbell

_____

_____

_____

51

What if this very moment was exactly why you were
alive? What would you do with it?

_____

_____

_____

The way you live should be the purest expression of your life's message.

Joseph Ranseth
Go ahead, start a movement.

Share the AHA messages from this book socially by going to
http://aha.pub/StartAMovement.

Section III

Your Big Idea

Every great leader who started a movement was first illumined by a Big Idea. Bigger than simply a new innovation, or an insight that hits you in the shower, a true Big Idea is an expression of a spiritual truth and has the power to bring people together under a common cause.

Through this section, take some time to connect to the truths that have shaped you, and how they may be a part of your movement.

52

A true Big Idea is bigger than you. It reaches beyond self-interest.

53

Have you found a Big Idea that you're willing to work toward your whole life?

_____

_____

_____

54

The world doesn't need *another* unique selling proposition. It needs Big Ideas that inspire the world to be a better place.

_____

_____

_____

55

A goal is something that shows up in the physical world. A Big Idea is the eternal principle that drives action and inspires the goals.

_____

_____

_____

56

To find a true Big Idea, you have to lift your gaze higher
than how it will serve you or what you will get.
A true Big Idea serves all.

_____

_____

_____

57

Your Big Idea isn't just about forsaking self interest, it's
adopting something that serves a much
larger portion of the planet.

_____

_____

_____

58

A person with low self-esteem can be completely wrapped up in the well-being of another person, but that doesn't make them a saint. It makes them co-dependent.

_____

_____

_____

59

Your Big Idea requires you to operate from your greatness, so people can see its expression in you.

_____

_____

_____

60

Are you willing to live -- and even give -- your life for your Big Idea if need be? Until you say yes, your greatest power is still untapped.

_____

_____

_____

61

Is your Big Idea inspiring enough to keep you going when the going gets tough?

_____

_____

_____

62

If you can throw in the towel at the first sign of adversity, you haven't tapped into the power of a Big Idea that can change the world -- yet.

_____

_____

_____

63

Would you celebrate the achievement of your Big Idea
even if you didn't get any credit for it?

_____

_____

_____

64

If you're looking for credit, your gaze isn't focused where it needs to be to make your movement happen.

_____

_____

_____

65

When your focus is on a true Big Idea,
you are more concerned with standing up for what's
right than you are with standing out from others.

_____

_____

_____

66

Once you embrace the Big Idea that drives your movement, you'll stop pointing fingers and start holding hands.

_____

_____

_____

67

Truth thinks in terms of "we" and "us," not "me" and "you." Your movement will unite people, not divide them.

_____

_____

_____

68

A Big Idea has the power to change people's behavior because it transforms the way they see the world.

_____

_____

_____

69

A Big Idea doesn't just inspire admiration from afar, it makes people feel included.

_____

_____

_____

70

All people want to be a part of something bigger than themselves. Your movement will unite people around a Big Idea that serves all.

_____

_____

_____

71

A Big Idea is like a bridge. It connects what was
previously disconnected.

_____

_____

_____

72

A true Big Idea allows differences to exist.
Our differences may make us distinct,
but they don't need to divide us.

_____

_____

_____

73

Your Big Idea shouldn't homogenize people, it should bring them together with love and acceptance.

_____

_____

_____

74

We are all in this together. What you do affects me, what I do affects you. A Big Idea recognizes and honors this truth.

_____

_____

_____

75

Movements that make the world better are not exclusive. They positively impact all, not just those who embrace it.

_____

_____

_____

76

Every great movement was built on a Big Idea that in one way or another, expressed the timeless truth that we are all one.

_____

_____

_____

Every great **movement** was preceded by a unifying **Big Idea.**

What's yours?

Joseph Ranseth
Go ahead, start a movement.

Share the AHA messages from this book socially by going to
http://aha.pub/StartAMovement.

Section IV

A Clear Message

A Clear Message is the expression of your Big Idea and is the way to transmit your Big Idea to the hearts and minds of your audience. When you see a picture of Dr. King, you think of his timeless words: "I have a dream. . ." We may not know every word of that speech, but we know the essence. This was his Clear Message.

How can you communicate your Big Idea so people can easily see its power? That's your Clear Message.

77

When people see a picture of Martin Luther King Jr., they think: "I have a dream." What do they think of when they see you?

_____

_____

_____

78

A Clear Message explains in very few words
what could easily occupy a library.

_____

_____

_____

79

An effective message is presented in a way that everyone can understand, not just in their head but also in their heart.

_____

_____

_____

80

Your message should articulate your Big Idea in a way that transcends the perceived barriers between people.

_____

_____

_____

81

Words have the power to unite previously separated people for a larger cause.

_____

_____

_____

82

Before you build anything in your business, you have just your words -- and words are enough to inspire people to action.

83

A well-designed message will associate with something that your audience experiences on a regular basis. This will create a trigger to remind them of your Big Idea.

_____

_____

_____

84

Voting stations in churches tend to skew more conservatively. Wine stores that play French music sell more French wine. What reminds people of your movement?

_____

_____

_____

85

Analogies make ideas and concepts easier to remember. What analogy embodies your Big Idea?

_____

_____

_____

86

Be bold and unexpected. If you catch people off guard, you will catch their attention. Then, make sure to deliver.

_____

_____

_____

87

Craft your message so it creates a natural curiosity gap. A mind that works for something will remember it.

_____

_____

_____

88

Your Big Idea can be an abstract concept;
your Clear Message should be concrete.

_____

_____

_____

89

A Big Idea is spiritual in nature; the Clear Message is
what embodies it in the physical world.

_____

_____

_____

90

If a Big Idea is true, then the Clear Message should present as self-evident.

_____

_____

_____

91

All human beings have the same core drives: safety, novelty, to feel significant, to be connected, to grow, and to contribute. The more drives your message hits, the more likely it will spread.

_____

_____

_____

92

Can your Clear Message make people feel special while also allowing them to feel connected to others?

_____

_____

_____

93

High-arousal emotions cause things to spread.
Positive high-arousal emotions spread positivity.

_____

_____

_____

94

A true Clear Message can be demonstrated by visible
action that others can emulate for themselves.

_____

_____

_____

95

When people look at you, can they see your transformation without you needing to explain it with words?

_____

_____

_____

96

Use as many words as necessary, but use your example more than you use your words.

_____

_____

_____

Everybody wants to be a part of something bigger than themselves.

Give them that opportunity.

Joseph Ranseth

Go ahead, start a movement.

Share the AHA messages from this book socially by going to
http://aha.pub/StartAMovement.

Section V

An Army of Advocates

No movement spreads all on its own. Every Big Idea needs evangelists to carry that movement forward. Your Army of Advocates are those relationships you have and the community you build that willingly and passionately embody the Big Idea behind your movement and take that message to the world.

It's not about the numbers, it's about uniting people who want to create an impact.

97

Your movement is bigger than you, so you're going to need an army of advocates for the cause.

_____

_____

_____

98

It wouldn't have done Gandhi or Dr. King any good to march by themselves; it is the community that creates power.

_____

_____

_____

99

Your Evangelists should be able to adopt your Big Idea without needing to give up their identity in the process.

_____

_____

_____

100

Finding someone who buys in to your Big Idea is far more valuable than someone who buys your product.

_____

_____

_____

101

If someone buys your product, you have them for a moment. If someone buys into your Big Idea, you have them for a lifetime.

_____

_____

_____

102

A true leader isn't looking for followers; they empower others to pick up the cause for themselves.

_____

_____

_____

103

Marketing attempts to change someone's behavior, but a movement changes the way people see the world.

_____

_____

_____

104

If we compromise our values for the sake of gaining a fan, we've sold ourselves short and sold out on our Big Idea.

_____

_____

_____

105

Instead of searching for the path of least resistance, embrace the path of greatest influence.

_____

_____

_____

106

Marketing often seeks to enslave people to their emotions. A movement has the power to liberate people from them.

_____

_____

_____

107

Your movement will not only bring people together,
it will inspire the best in them.

_____

_____

_____

108

Your movement will do more than simply get people to
take action, it will change them from the inside out.

_____

_____

_____

109

The true essence of being spiritual is to see and be driven by something that transcends us as individuals and unites us to the rest of humanity.

_____

_____

_____

110

Simple things done for a noble, unifying purpose can create great impact.

_____

_____

_____

111

You can sell someone a product and you'll have their money, but if you help someone see the greatness within themselves, you'll have their heart.

_____

_____

_____

112

Your movement doesn't need a million people to change the world; there is great power in simply having two or more minds united in a single cause.

_____

_____

_____

113

The success of your movement is not in the number of people who follow you, but in the number of lives changed for the better.

_____

_____

_____

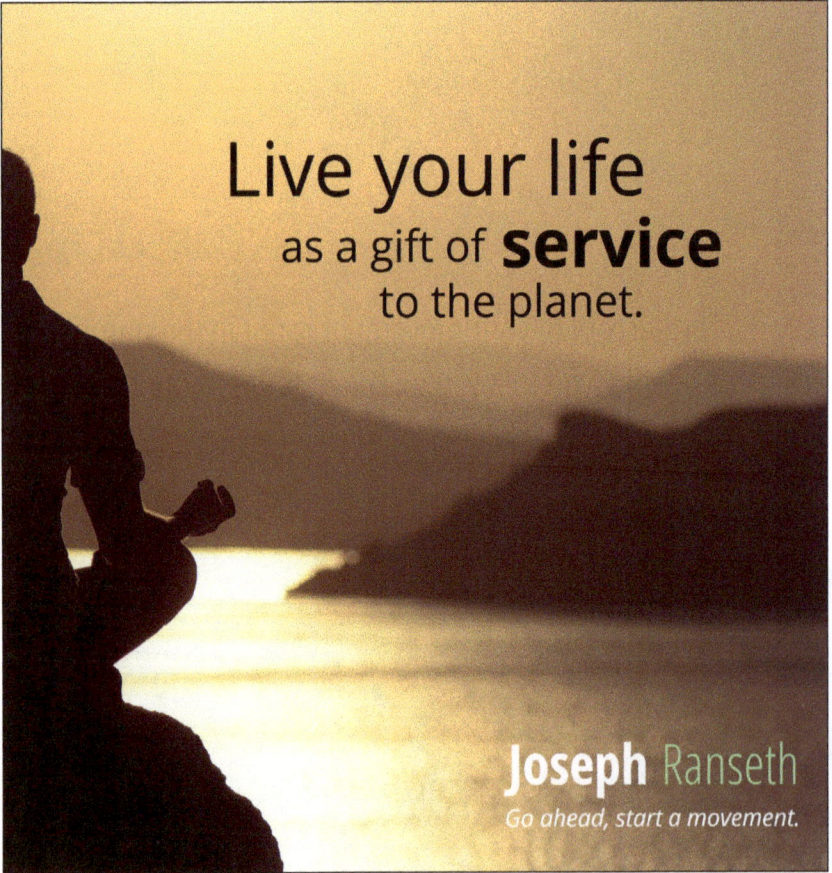

Live your life
as a gift of **service**
to the planet.

Joseph Ranseth

Go ahead, start a movement.

Share the AHA messages from this book socially by going to
http://aha.pub/StartAMovement.

Section VI

Finding Your Zero

Adversity is what qualifies you for your movement. The Big Idea, the Clear Message, and the Army of Advocates are the blueprint on how to architect your movement. Element Zero is the fuel that activates the power of your movement. Without it, your movement will never achieve the level of transformation that it could.

When asked the secret of his power, Gandhi said it was because he made himself "zero." It's time to find your zero.

114

When asked the secret of his power, Gandhi answered: "I strive to make myself zero." We unlock a power available to us all when our efforts are no longer about our own selfish gain.

_____

_____

_____

115

What we do matters, but not nearly as much as why we do it.

_____

_____

_____

116

Just as we grow from dependence, to independence, to interdependence, so should our desires evolve beyond ourselves to the well-being of others and the world as a whole.

117

What consumes your mind, controls your life.

118

To the mind that asks "how may I serve?" in each moment, a movement can spark from the humblest of places.

_____

_____

_____

119

It's not just our attachments we need to let go of,
it's also our aversions.

_____

_____

_____

120

The end does not justify the means. The means create the end. Let each action remain as pure as your Big Idea.

_____

_____

_____

121

Gandhi didn't ever say: "Be the change you want to see in the world." Find out what he really said: JosephRanseth.com/gandhi

_____

_____

_____

122

If you had no words to speak, would your life still change others?

_____

_____

_____

123

Your presence alone, when living aligned with your Big Idea, will liberate others and inspire them to see their true nature.

_____

_____

_____

124

Are you willing to give your life in the service of others?

_____

_____

_____

125

If you knew you would die tomorrow, how would you live today?

_____

_____

_____

126

Close your eyes and imagine your dream life 5 years from now. If your vision is not in what you can get, but how you can serve others, you may be ready to start a movement.

_____

_____

_____

127

Love is not a feeling of attachment, but a whole-hearted desire for the well-being of those we profess to love.

_____

_____

_____

128

When you are aligned with your purpose and source of power, you will be a person in whose presence others feel loved and empowered.

_____

_____

_____

129

Customers won't come to your funeral. People whose lives you changed will.

_____

_____

_____

130

When we see our own true nature, the need for external validation disappears.

_____

_____

_____

131

Our movement begins when we begin living for others.

_____

_____

_____

132

Let your life be fueled by love for humanity, and every day will be an expression of your movement.

_____

_____

_____

133

Those who have had the greatest impact on the planet for good have found a power only activated when the focus shifts outward in service to others.

_____

_____

_____

134

How would you live your life if your every daily need was supplied by a power greater than yourself?

_____

_____

_____

135

Our lives become transformational when we find a purpose greater than ourselves.

_____

_____

_____

136

When we live fully expressed in our true nature, it activates a recognition in others of their own true nature.

_____

_____

_____

137

Your liberation is a gift of service to humanity.

138

Until we go within, we go without.

_____

_____

_____

139

There is a journey each one of us is called on. It is a journey of meaning and impact. This journey is within.

_____

_____

_____

140

The deeper we go within ourselves, the greater the impact we can have on the world around us.

_____

_____

_____

About the Author

Joseph Ranseth

You have a movement within you; Joseph wants to help. As a speaker, author, and transformationist for over fifteen years, Joseph Ranseth has been helping people transform their lives and organizations using the same blueprint and principles that transformational leaders like Gandhi and Dr. King used to change the world. He has been a featured expert on national television, including Fox News, CBS, CTV, CBC, etc., in leading industry publications, such as Advertising Age, and has been recognized several times by the Huffington Post for using social media to inspire the world. A popular speaker, Joseph is the host of several events, including the Global Influence Summit, an annual event that helps speakers, authors, coaches, and purpose-driven entrepreneurs increase their reach and impact so they can take their movements to the world.

AHAthat™

AHAthat makes it easy to share, author, and promote content. There are over 40,000 quotes (AHAmessages™) by thought leaders from around the world that you can share in seconds for free.

For those who want to author their own book, we have time-tested proven processes that allow you to write your AHAbook™ of 140 digestible, bite-sized morsels in eight hours or less. Once your content is on AHAthat, you have a customized link that you can use to have your fans/advocates share your content and help grow your network.

➲ Start sharing: **https://AHAthat.com**

➲ Start authoring: **https://AHAthat.com/Author**

Hey,
Did You
AHAthat™?

Joseph Ranseth
AHAthat Author

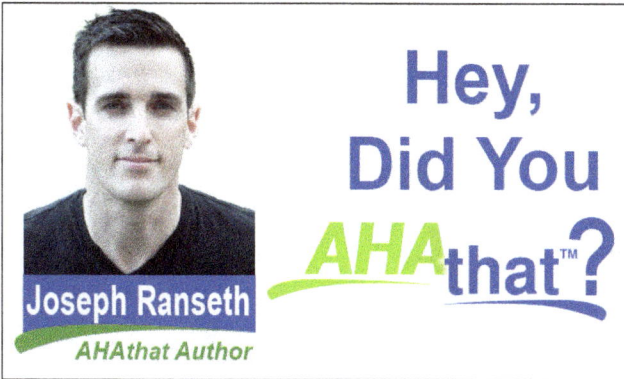

Please go directly to this book in AHAthat and share each AHAmessage socially at **http://aha.pub/StartAMovement**.